Mel Bay Presents

Favor
American
Polkas and Jigs

for Fiddle
By Stacy Phillips

MW00804594

1 2 3 4 5 6 7 8 9 0

© 2007 BY MEL BAY PUBLICATIONS, INC., PACIFIC, MO 63069.

Visit us on the Web at www.melbay.com — E-mail us at email@melbay.com

DISCOGRAPHY

For recordings of the fiddlers in this book:

County Sales
PO Box 191
Floyd, VA 24091
http://www.countysales.com/

Record Depot
PO Box 3057
Roanoke, VA 24015
ph: 540-343-5355

Labels that record a lot of traditional fiddling include:

Document
County
Rounder
Missouri State Old Time Fiddlers Assoc.
Voyager
Rebel
Yazoo
CMH

Try web searches for these labels and individual fiddlers and tunes.
Many current fiddlers distribute their own CD's.

Table of Contents

Introduction

This compilation is not meant to teach fiddle, but to serve as a reference to the fiddler's repertoire.

To keep the books within a reasonable size, I have limited myself to mostly public domain tunes played in one of the several standard, but ill-defined geographic styles of the United States; New England, Southeastern and Bluegrass, Midwestern, and Southwestern. I have omitted what might be loosely called "ethnic" styles.

This music was learned from recordings, fiddle contests, jam sessions, dances, and meetings with individual fiddlers. (I would like to thank Danny Gardella, Matt Glaser, Bill Christopherson, Kenny Kosek, Stuart Williams, Ruthie Dornfeld, Becky Miller, Paul Elliot, Tim O'Brien, Kerry Blech, Armin Barnett, Gere Canote, John Hartford, Tony Marcus, Ray Bierl, and Pete Sutherland for generously sharing their time.)

I experienced extensive soul searching when considering bowing. Slur patterns contribute mightily to a player's style, but even the repetition of a selection is often bowed differently. In addition, it is virtually impossible to transcribe phrasing from a raucous old string band recording with complete accuracy. Therefore I have tried to capture at least the bowings most critical to a tune's interpretation. A novice fiddler will be able to learn a lot about the parameters within which players define good or "authentic" playing by using the supplied bowing as a starting point. I think it is essential that players not familiar with all manner of regional styles to begin with the given notation. But since I erred on the side of caution when notating them, many of these tunes could use a couple more well placed slurs. Alternatively, after a long note, you can play the next note with the same bow direction to get it going in the same direction in which you feel most comfortable. This will be most easily applied to polkas which have many notes of long duration.

All of these versions are taken directly from the playing of well-established fiddlers. The name in parentheses following the title identifies the chief source of the setting. Those with two names are based either on two recordings, or less often, when the chosen version used two fiddlers. If the music was taken from a commercial recording on which the fiddler was not identified, the name of the artist credited on the label is given after the fiddler's name.

Tunes with no indicated source were either based on my own arrangement, or had too many influences to be untangled.

Different versions of the same tune are notated by capital letters in parentheses, following the title. When two completely different melodies have the same title, they are notated by number.

Though I have tried to choose interesting settings for each tune, it is not my hope that any become the standard version just because they are in a book. The same applies to the chord accompaniment. There are many interpretations that sound fine.

For more in-depth introduction to my collection of tunes, please see the introduction to Volume One of the The Phillips Collection of Traditional American Fiddle Tunes; Hoedowns, Breakdowns and Reels (MB94711).

Stacy Phillips
March, 2003

Acknowledgements

I wish to recognize the generous help of the following for access to their record collections, and their willingness to share their knowledge of old-time fiddle tunes.

Armin Barnett, Ed and Geraldine Berbaum, Ray Bierl, Kerry Blech, Martha Burns, Gere Canote, Barbara Collins, Stephen Davis, Jim Day, Bill Dillof, Ruthie Dornfeld, Julie Durell, Paul Elliot, Frank Ferrel, Danny Gardella, Matt Glaser, Skip Gorman, Hank Haley, John Hartford, Matthew Hartz, Peggy Harvey, Penny Hauser, Dave Howard, Judy Hyman, Ron Kane, Shirley Koehler and Family, Kenny Kosek, Rich Levine, Larry MacBride, Tony Marcus, Mel Marshall, Peter Martin, Meghan Merker, Gary Lee Moore, Dale Morris, Tim O'Brien, Mosheh Savitsky, Susan Steingold, Pete Sutherland, Becky Tracey, Phil and Vivian Williams, Stuart Williams, and Tim Woodbridge.

Ruthie Dornfeld, Ellen Cohn and Dave Howard for yeoman editing.

TO ALL THE GREAT FIDDLERS WHOSE MUSIC CREATED THIS BOOK

Reading the Music Notation

Most of the notation is standard. I have included a few symbols which are particularly useful for fiddle music.

There are two notations for slides. In both cases, do not change fingering or bow direction.

1. **E1** Slide from the first note to the second. These glissandi are usually quick. Half-step slides with this notation sometimes begin a bit sharper than the indicated pitch; i.e., the slide may actually be a bit less than indicated.

2. **E2** This indicates a short (usually not more than a half-step), quick slide, either up or down. The pitch at the beginning of the slide has no duration.

When there are more than two sections in a piece, they are indicated by numbers—enclosed in rectangles. When there is an apostrophe after the section number (eg: 2'), it indicates an alternative version of that part.

The capital letters above the staff represent only one of many acceptable alternatives for chords. Occasional alternate or optional choices appear in parentheses.

The small numbers in parentheses that occasionally appear over the staff indicate fingering.

In jigs, the typical series of three eighth notes shown in example E3 is often phrased closer to that shown in example E4—or, less often as shown in example E5 (or somewhere between these extremes).

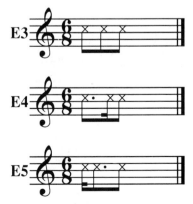

Polkas

ALLENTOWN POLKA (Mark O'Connor)

BEER BARREL POLKA (Robert Wise)

8

BOYS AROUND THE WORLD (Cyril Stinnett)

BRAHMS POLKA (Vivian Williams)

THE BUGLE BLOWS, THE TRUMPET BLOWS (Jehile Kirkhuff)

This version was unaccompanied. Play section 3 four times.

CALGARY POLKA (Mark O'Connor)

CHATEAU GAI (Bill Christopherson and Tom Phillips with the Fish Family)

a.k.a. "Chateagaie"

CHURCH STREET POLKA (Pete Sutherland)

CHEROKEE POLKA (Ed Haley)

CHURNING BUTTER (Hugh Farr and Ed Newman)

CLARINET POLKA (A) (Mark O'Connor)

The order of sections is 1-2-1-3-1.

16

CLARINET POLKA (B)

The order of sections is 1-2-1-3-1.

COW ACROSS THE ROAD (Hugh Farr)

CROOKED STOVE PIPE (Vivian Williams)

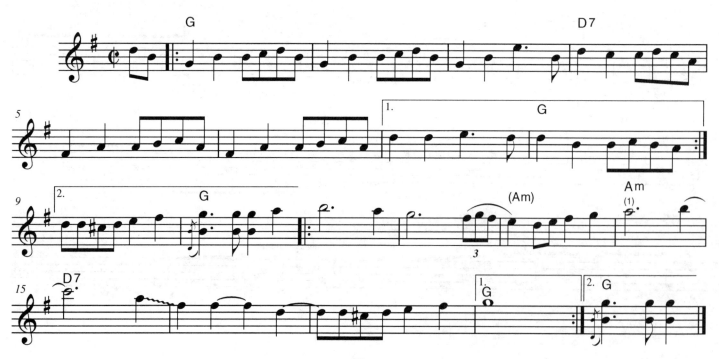

D AND A POLKA (Jehile Kirkhuff)

a.k.a. "The Quadrille Polka"

FLORIDA POLKA (Robert Wise)

FOGGY VALLEY (Mary Trotchie)

GILES ROY POLKA (Henry Landry)

HELENA POLKA (Vivian Williams)

HAPPY ACRES (Vivian Williams)

HELVETIA POLKA (Argel Kaufman)

a.k.a. "Poor Uncle Davy" and "Rochester Schottische"
This is a polka version of "Military Schottische."

HOPSCOTCH POLKA (Harvey Taylor)

This version was unaccompanied.

JENNIE LIND POLKA (Kenny Baker)

JESSIE POLKA

26

LICHTENSTEINER POLKA (Jehile Kirkhuff)

MOON BEHIND THE MOUNTAIN (Jim Childress with Uncle Henry's Favorites)

PUMPKIN VINE (Jimmy Wheeler)

RICHMOND POLKA (Clark Kessinger)

a.k.a. "Green Mountain Polka" and "Plaza Polka"
This is a polka version of "Richmond Cotillion."

SAY NO MORE (by Mark Simos (Bill Christopherson and Tom Phillips with the Fish Family))

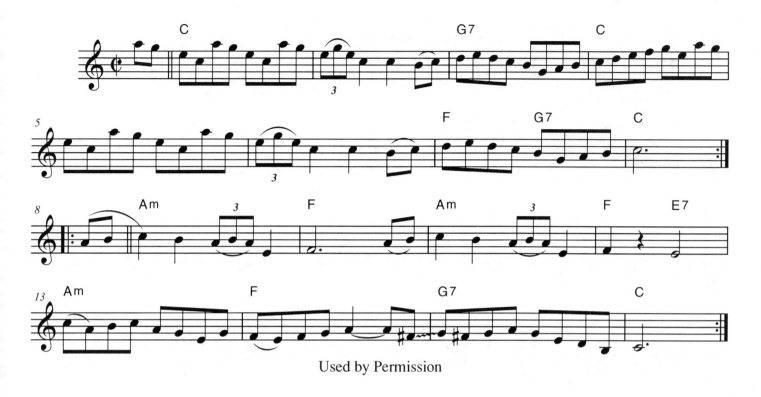

Used by Permission

SPRUCETOPPER'S POLKA (Stuart Williams)

TOPEKA POLKA (Donnell Cooley and Tim Hodgson)

Play section 1 four times.

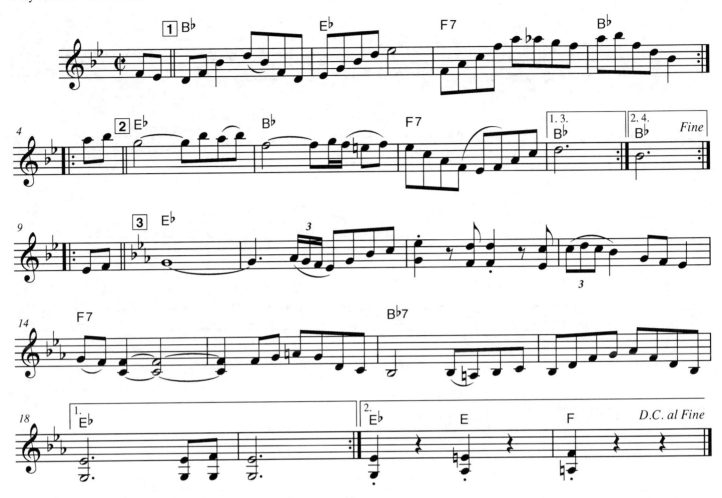

WEST VIRGINIA POLKA (Lynn Smith)

WINTER FLOWER POLKA (Forrest Daugherty)

YEAR OF THE JUBILO by Henry Clay Work

a.k.a. "Jubilo"

YORK COUNTY (Ben Guilmette)

BALTZELL'S TUNE (Rollie Hammon)

BIG MAC JIG

BLUEBERRY JIG (Stuart Williams)

BOX STOVE JIG (Clem Myers)

a.k.a. "The Old Box Stove"

BRIDE OF THE WINDS (Stuart Williams)

CAPTAIN JINKS (Don Woodcock)

CAT IN THE HOPPER (Ruthie Dornfeld)

This version was unaccompanied.

THE CHAMPION

Some people play the second section with C naturals instead of sharps and substituting C chords for A7.

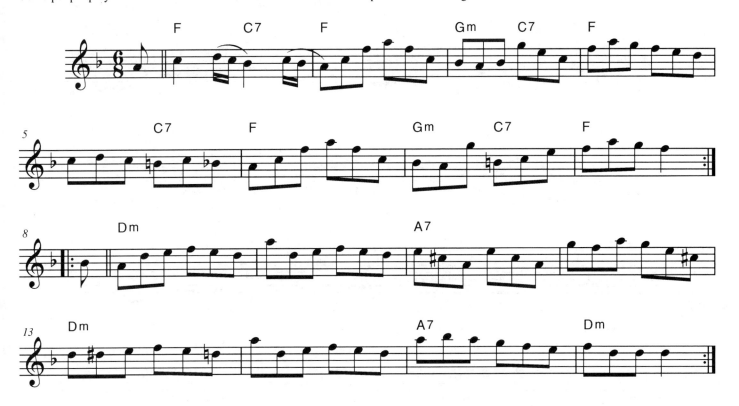

CHARLIE HUNTER'S JIG (Pete Sutherland)

This version was unaccompanied.

CIRCLE JIG (New Hampshire Fiddler's Union)

COWBOY JIG (Rodney Miller)

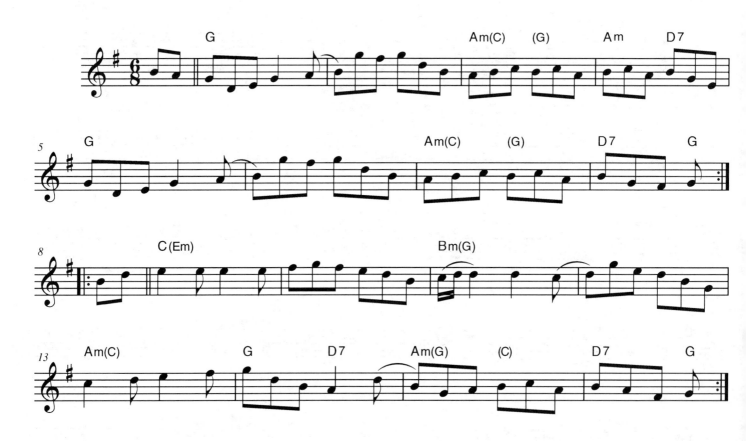

THE ESSENCE OF SUGAR CANE (Jehile Kirkhuff)

Play section 1 four times. This version was unaccompanied.
This is related to "Darkie's Dream" in Favorite American Rags & Blues for Fiddle (MB20581).

FAIR JENNY'S JIG by Peter Barnes © 1976 (Pete Sutherland)

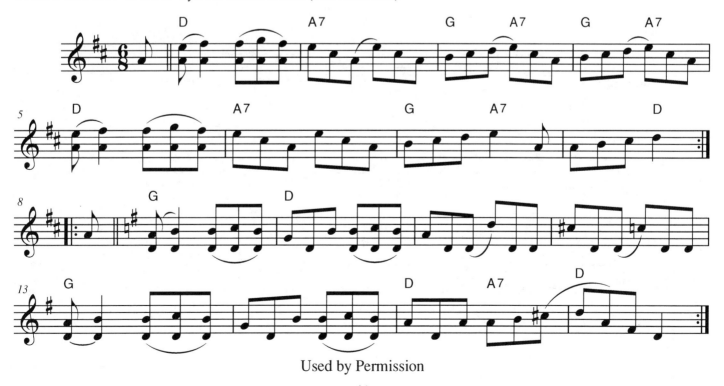

Used by Permission

FORT GARY JIG (Stuart Williams and Al DeLorme)

GARY OWENS

GOLDEN TRESSES (Jehile Kirkhuff)

Play section 1 four times. This version was unaccompanied. This may work best as a hornpipe.

HASTE TO THE WEDDING (Jehile Kirkhuff)

HOBO JIG

HONEST JOHN (Vivian Williams)

IRISHMAN'S HEART TO THE LADIES (A) (Stuart Williams and Wayne Holmes)

IRISHMAN'S HEART TO THE LADIES (B) (Ruthie Dornfeld)

a.k.a. "Irishman's Farewell" and "Sweet Biddy Daley"

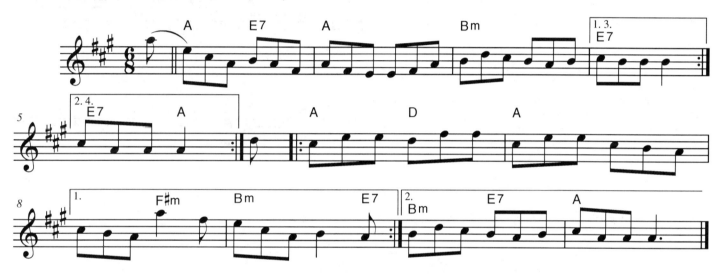

JOHNSON'S ROAD (Lawrence Older)

This version was unaccompanied.

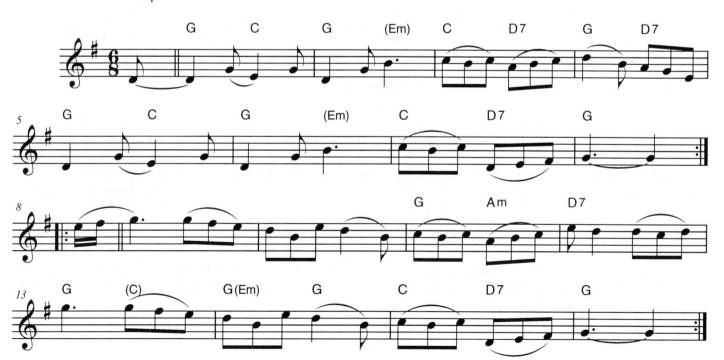

KELTON'S JIG (Jehile Kirkhuff)

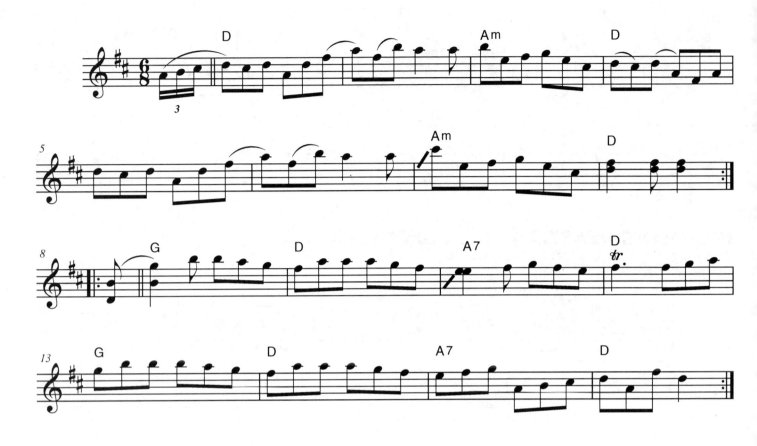

KITTY McGEE (Pete Sutherland with The Arm and Hammer String Band)

LAD O'BEIRNE'S JIG (Becky Miller)

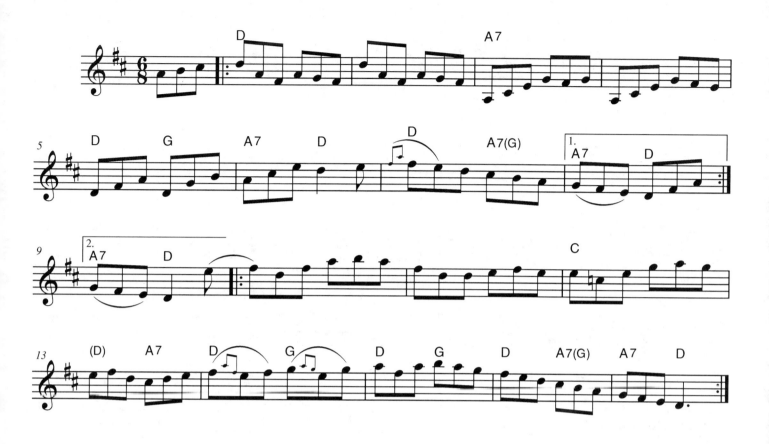

LARRY O'GAFF (Jehile Kirkhuff)
a.k.a. "O'Gaff's Jig"

LITTLE BURNT POTATO

MAGGIE BROWN'S FAVORITE

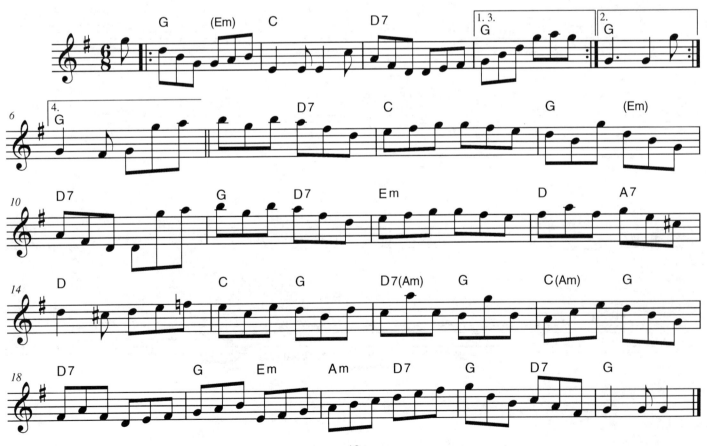

MOUTH OF THE POTOMAC (Jehile Kirkhuff)

This is a jig version of the reel titled "Mouth of the Tobique." This version was unaccompanied.

NAOMI'S JIG (Ben Guillemette)

NEW RIGGED SHIP (Vivian Williams)

This is a jig version of "Green Willis" in The Phillips Collection of Traditional American Fiddle Tunes Vol 1. (MB94711).
a.k.a. "Old Lady in the Haymow" and "Two Step Quadrille."

OFF SHE GOES 2 (Everett Douglas)

THE OLD RED BARN (Down Rowan)

Play the D7 chord in parentheses on the second and fourth repetitions.

OLD FIGARY~O (John Francis)

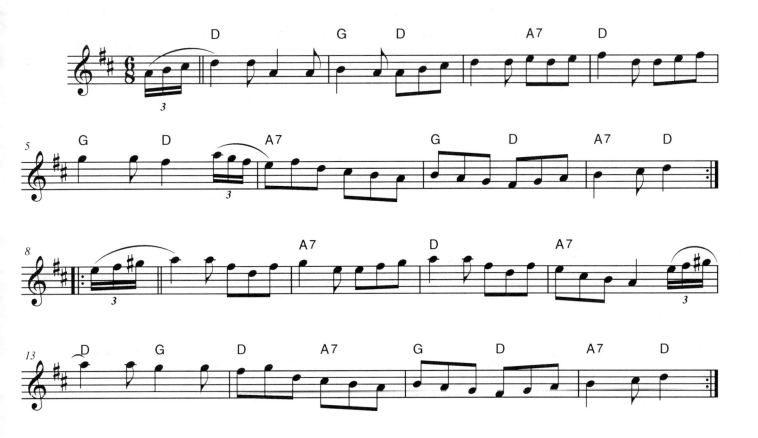

OVER THE GARDEN WALL (Harvey Taylor)

This version was unaccompanied.

51

PADDY WACK (Jehile Kirkhuff)

a.k.a. "Little Peg's Jig."

PERRY'S VICTORY (Wilhemina Scott)

Add A drones to the first section. This version was unaccompanied.

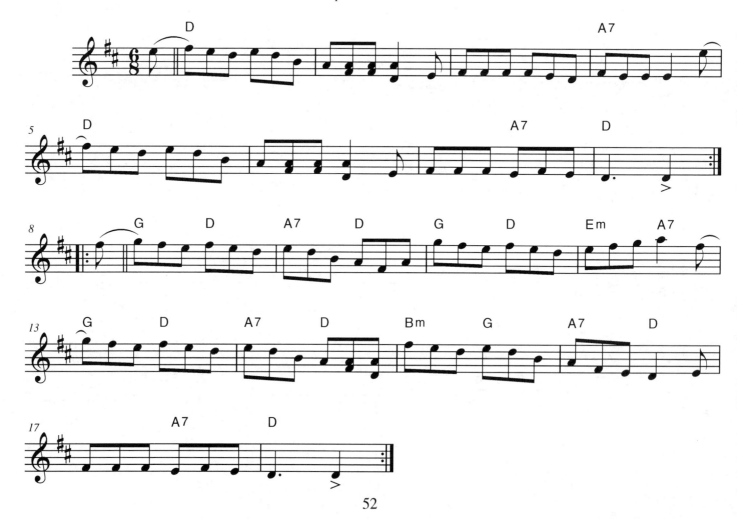

PLYMOUTH LASSES (Donald Woodcock)

PORTLAND FANCY JIG (The Plymouth Old Time Dance Orchestra)

THE ROAD TO SKYE (Donna Herbert)

a.k.a. "Kitty of Coleraine"

ROCK VALLEY JIG (Clem Myers)

RORY O'MOORE (Pete Sutherland)

SAILOR'S WIFE (Kerry Elkin with Tradition Today)

SAINT LAWRENCE JIG (Donna White Reed)

SILVER LAKE QUADRILLE (Bob Walters)

This version was unaccompanied.

SMASH THE WINDOWS (Danny Gardella)

a.k.a. "Roaring Jelly Jig"

STOOL OF REPENTANCE (Becky Tracy)

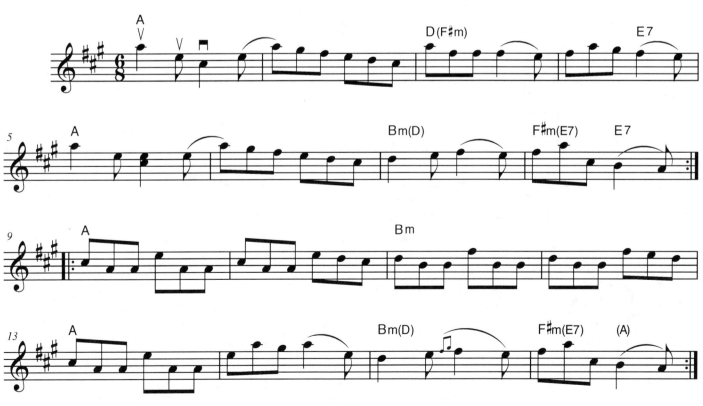

SWALLOW TAIL JIG (Tom McCreesh with Fennig's All Star String Band)

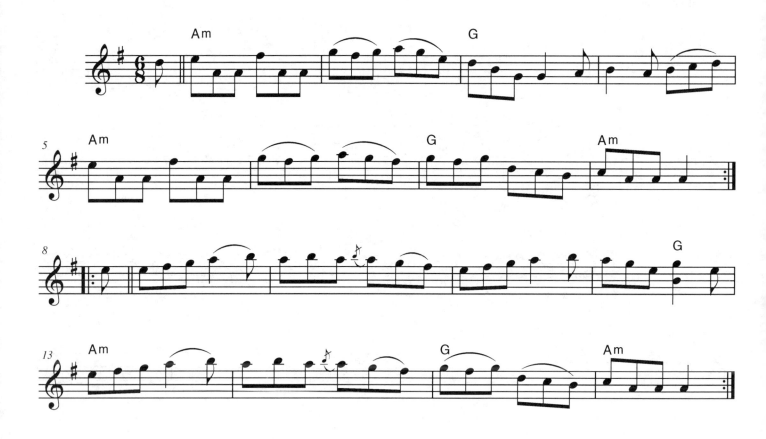

TEVIOT JIG (Ron West)

a.k.a. "Tiviot Jig"
The G natural is often played sharp with an accompanying E7 chord.

THOMPSON'S JIG (Angus Chisolm and Mosheh Savitsky)
a.k.a. "The Frost is All Over"

TOBIN'S JIG (Author)
a.k.a. "Tobin's Favorite" and "Tobin's Fancy"

TOP OF THE ROAD (Becky Tracy)
a.k.a. "High Part of the Road"

TRIPPING UP THE STAIRS

TRIP TO THE COTTAGE (Don Woodcock and Dave Howard)

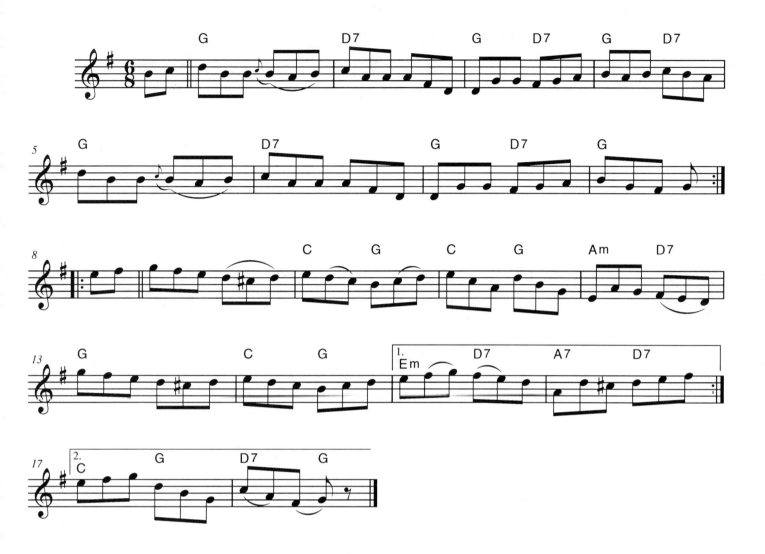

UNTITLED JIG I

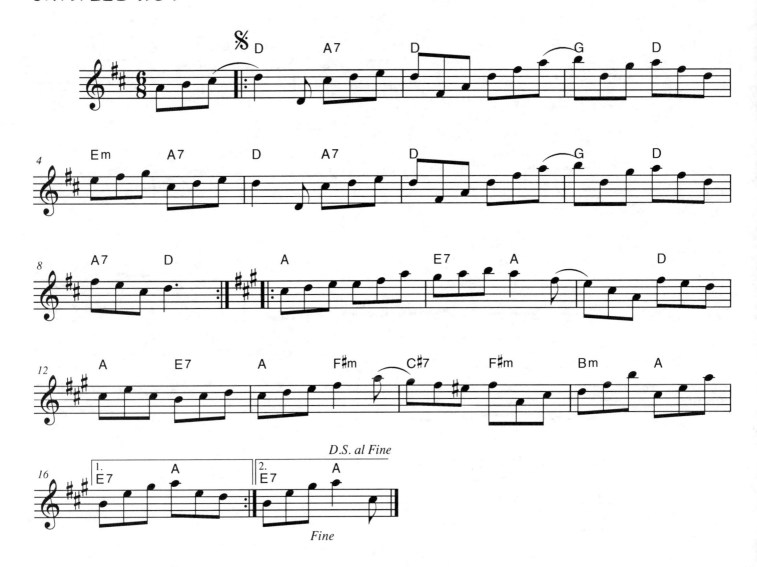

NOTES

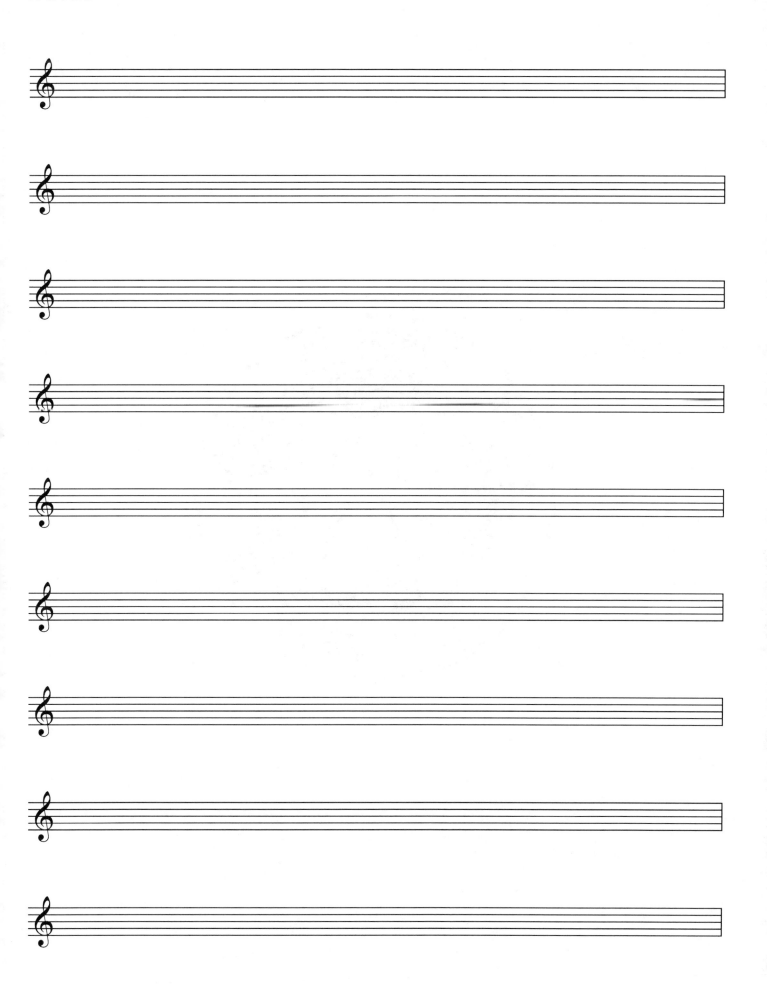